Maze Craze
Pirate Mazes

Don-Oliver Matthies

Sterling Publishing Co., Inc.
New York

Library of Congress Cataloging-in-Publication Data Available

10   9   8   7   6

Published in 2003 by Sterling Publishing Co., Inc.
387 Park Avenue South
New York, NY 10016
Originally published in Germany in 2002 under the title *Der Schatz
der Piraten* by Edition Bücherbär im Arena Verlag GmbH
Wurzburg, Germany
© 2002 by Arena Verlag GmbH
English translation © 2003 by Sterling Publishing Co., Inc.
Distributed in Canada by Sterling Publishing
c/o Canadian Manda Group
One Atlantic Avenue, Suite 105
Toronto, Ontario, M6K 3E7, Canada
Distributed in Great Britain and Europe by Chris Lloyd at Orca Book
Services, Stanley House, Fleets Lane, Poole BH15 3AJ, England
Distributed in Australia by Capricorn Link (Australia) Pty. Ltd.
P.O. Box 704, Windsor, NSW 2756, Australia

Sterling ISBN 1-4027-0603-0

Maze Craze
Pirate Mazes

Draw a picture or
place a photograph of
yourself here.

This book belongs to:

_____

This is Captain Silver. He is a
famous pirate. When he is not
capturing ships, he enjoys
solving mazes.

Early in the morning after a long pirate party, Captain Silver makes his way to his ship. Can you find the way through all the tables and benches?

The pirates have docked their boats in shallow water. How can Captain Silver find the way to his ship through the planks?

Now he has to climb the ropes to get on board. Unfortunately, they are all tangled. Can you untangle them for Captain Silver?

start

end

In the hold, the mice make themselves very comfortable.

In Captain Silver's quarters, all of his precious maze maps are lying around. Can you solve them?

Even in the ship's kitchen, the mice are having fun. Can you direct the hungry mouse to the cheese?

Captain Silver prepares to set sail, but he first has to solve the mazes on the sails!

In his cabin, Captain Silver studies ocean charts in order to see where he can seize a ship that is hopefully carrying tons of gold. Which ship is heading toward Treasure Island?

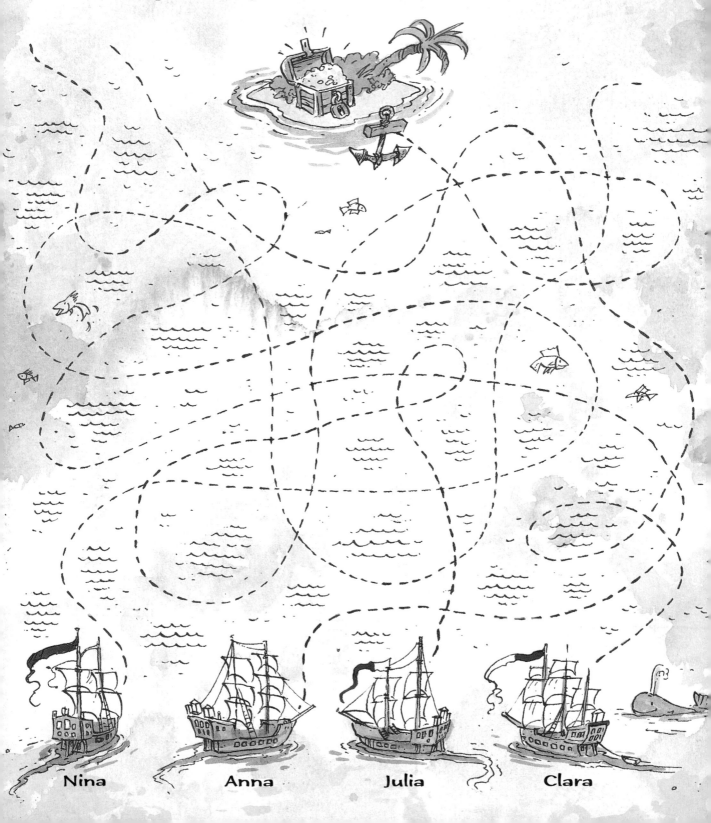

Nina   **Anna**   **Julia**   **Clara**

Fish are swimming underneath Captain Silver's ship. Can you direct the seahorse to the pearl?

Captain Silver finds a bottle with a treasure map inside. Which arrow leads to the gold, the red or the yellow?

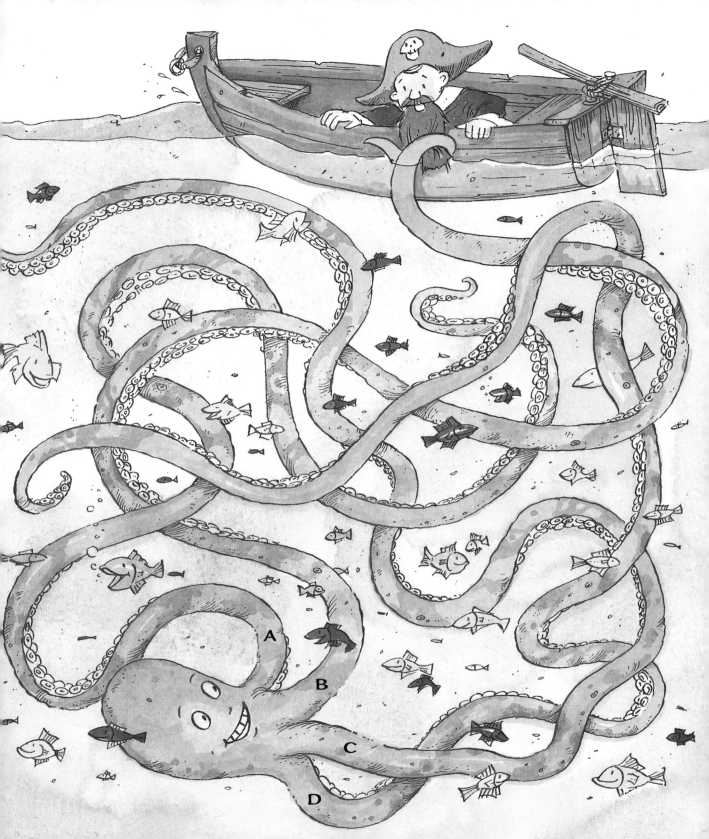

As Captain Silver is fishing, a friendly octopus begins to tease him. Which tentacle is holding onto Captain Silver's beard?

Exhausted from so many adventures, Captain Silver decides to take his afternoon nap. He dreams about mazes—can you solve this one?

When he wakes up, Captain Silver climbs on top of the crow's nest and looks for ships carrying gold. "What's that on the horizon?" he asks himself.

end

start

Captain Silver spots a huge ship. He climbs on board and sees that the crew is having a party. He can now sneak around and try to find the treasure, but he needs your help!

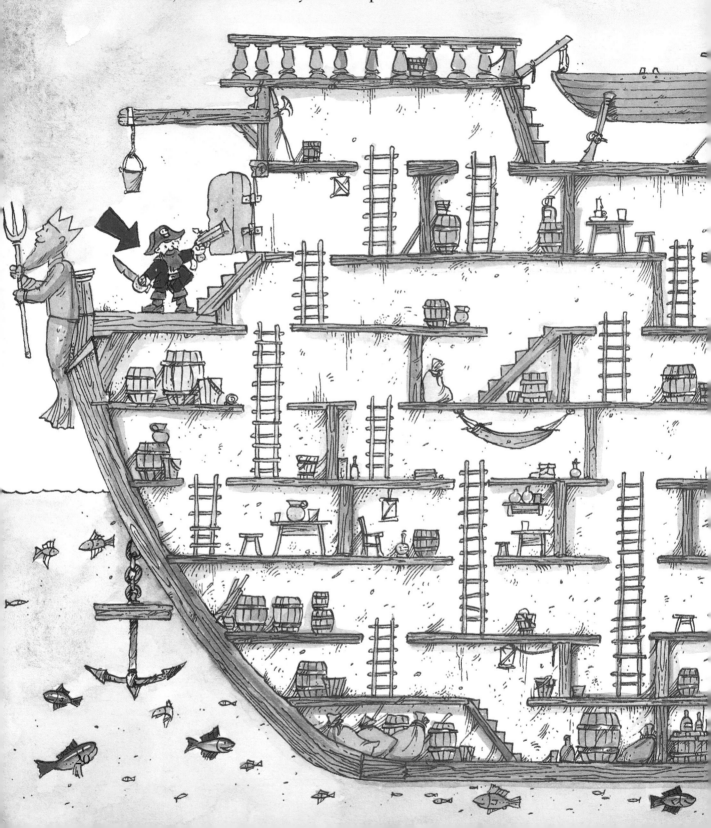

treasure

Unfortunately, Captain Silver only finds a couple of gold coins on the ship. However, he discovers a hidden treasure map of an old, forgotten Incan pyramid.

end

start

Captain Silver quickly sets out on his adventure to find the Incan pyramid. He is so excited about finding the possible treasure that everything around him turns into mazes, even the clouds!

Captain Silver is lost in the Mangrove Marshes. How can he get out?

end

start

After Captain Silver gets out of the marshes, he enters the jungle where huge, hungry pythons greet him. Luckily, he has some food to give them. Can you untangle the pythons' bodies?

As he goes deeper and deeper into the jungle, Captain Silver discovers a giant stone statue. Can you help him get inside?

end

start

"I'm never going to find the Incan pyramid," Captain Silver says to himself. He climbs a tree to get his bearings and suddenly sees the pyramid in the distance!

end

start

27

When Captain Silver reaches the pyramid, he spots a hole. "Is this the entrance?" he wonders. Do you see the path to the treasure?

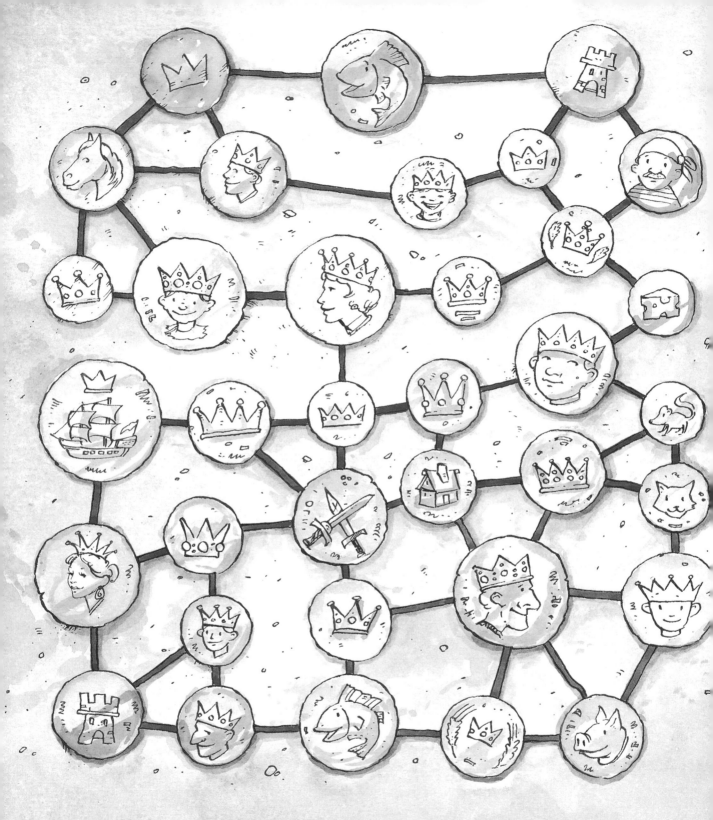

After Captain Silver finds the gold, he plays a little game with the coins. How can he go from the bottom fish coin to the top fish coin by only using the gold coins with crowns?

Captain Silver hides the treasures in his coat and makes his way back to the ship.

Captain Silver is so happy when he reaches his ship that he begins to sing a pirate song. Can you solve the maze in the moon?

Captain Silver and his pirate friends have a huge party to celebrate his discovery. He couldn't have found the treasure without your help!

Thank you!!

start

end

Answers

page 6

page 7

page 8

A=3
B=4
C=1
D=2

page 9

page 10

page 11

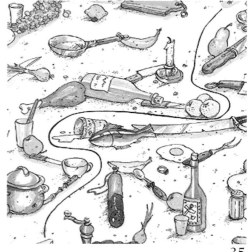

page 17

B

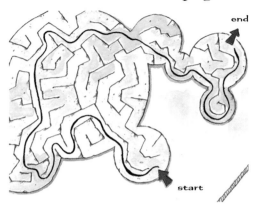

page 19

pages 20–21

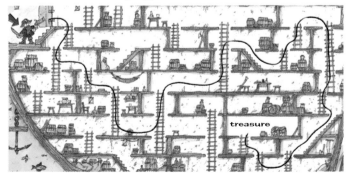

page 22

page 23

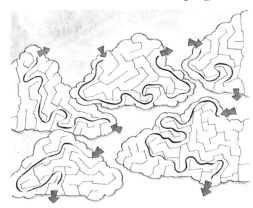

page 24

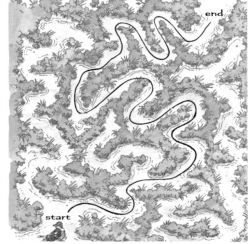

page 25

A=4
B=3
C=1
D=2

38

pages 28–29

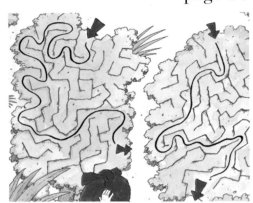

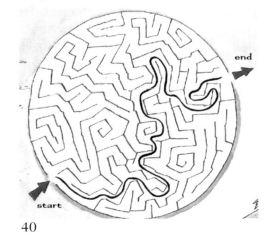